anythink

American Holidays
MARTIN LUTHER KING JR. DAY
Connor Dayton

PowerKiDS press.

New York

Published in 2012 by The Rosen Publishing Group, Inc.
29 East 21st Street, New York, NY 10010

First Edition

Editor: Jennifer Way
Book Design: Julio Gil

Photo Credits: Cover, p. 19 Jewel Samad/AFP/Getty Images; p. 5 Susan Stocker/South Florida Sun Sentinel/MCT via Getty Images; pp. 7, 17 Rolls Press/Popperfoto/Getty Images; pp. 9, 24 (bottom) Francis Miller/Time & Life Pictures/Getty Images; p. 11 Don Cravens/Time & Life Pictures/Getty Images; pp. 13, 24 (top left) William Lovelace/Express/Getty Images; pp. 14–15 Hulton Archive/Getty Images; pp. 21, 24 (top right) Jim West/age fotostock; p. 23 Alex Wong/Getty Images.

Library of Congress Cataloging-in-Publication Data

Dayton, Connor.
 Martin Luther King Jr. Day / by Connor Dayton. — 1st ed.
     p. cm. — (American holidays)
 Includes index.
 ISBN 978-1-4488-6144-6 (library binding) — ISBN 978-1-4488-6246-7 (pbk.) — ISBN 978-1-4488-6247-4 (6-pack)
 1. Martin Luther King, Jr., Day—Juvenile literature. 2. King, Martin Luther, Jr., 1929–1968—Juvenile literature. I. Title.
 E185.97.K5D36 2012
 394.261—dc23
                                    2011023443

Manufactured in the United States of America

CPSIA Compliance Information: Batch #WW12PK: For Further Information contact Rosen Publishing, New York, New York at 1-800-237-9932

Contents

A Great Leader 4

King's Life 6

Honoring King 18

Words to Know 24

Index 24

Web Sites 24

Martin Luther King Jr. Day is the third Monday in January. It honors a great American leader.

Martin Luther King Jr. was born on January 15, 1929. He was born in Atlanta, Georgia.

King spoke out against laws that were unfair to African Americans. He helped change these laws.

The work to change these unfair laws is called the civil rights movement.

King wanted people to work for civil rights peacefully.

King was known for leading **marches**. His biggest march was the March on Washington in 1963.

15

King was known for
his **speeches**, too. His best-
known speech is his
"I have a dream" speech.

Martin Luther King Jr. Day honors King. It honors civil rights, too.

People spend the holiday as a day of **service**.
This means doing things to help your community.

21

How do you celebrate Martin Luther King Jr. Day?

Words to Know

march

service

speech

Index

C
civil rights, 12, 18

L
laws, 8, 10

P
people, 12, 20

S
service, 20
speech(es), 16

Web Sites

Due to the changing nature of Internet links, PowerKids Press has developed an online list of Web sites related to the subject of this book. This site is updated regularly. Please use this link to access the list:
www.powerkidslinks.com/amh/king/